Tucholsky Wagner Zola Scott Sydow Freud Schlegel
Turgenev Wallace Fonatne Twain Walther von der Vogelweide Fouqué Friedrich II. von Preußen
Weber Freiligrath Kant Ernst Frey
Fechner Fichte Weiße Rose von Fallersleben Hölderlin Richthofen Frommel
Engels Fielding Eichendorff Tacitus Dumas
Fehrs Faber Flaubert Eliasberg Ebner Eschenbach
Feuerbach Maximilian I. von Habsburg Fock Eliot Zweig Vergil
Ewald London
Goethe Elisabeth von Österreich
Mendelssohn Balzac Shakespeare Dostojewski Ganghofer
Trackl Lichtenberg Rathenau Doyle Gjellerup
Stevenson Hambruch
Mommsen Tolstoi Lenz Droste-Hülshoff
Thoma Hanrieder
Dach Verne von Arnim Hägele Hauff Humboldt
Reuter Rousseau Hagen Hauptmann Gautier
Karrillon Garschin Defoe Baudelaire
Damaschke Descartes Hebbel
Hegel Kussmaul Herder
Wolfram von Eschenbach Dickens Schopenhauer
Bronner Darwin Melville Grimm Jerome Rilke George
Campe Horváth Aristoteles Bebel Proust
Bismarck Vigny Barlach Voltaire Federer Herodot
Gengenbach Heine
Storm Casanova Tersteegen Grillparzer Georgy
Chamberlain Lessing Langbein Gilm Gryphius
Brentano Lafontaine
Strachwitz Claudius Schiller Kralik Iffland Sokrates
Bellamy Schilling
Katharina II. von Rußland Gerstäcker Raabe Gibbon Tschechow
Löns Hesse Hoffmann Gogol Wilde Gleim Vulpius
Luther Heym Hofmannsthal Morgenstern
Roth Klee Hölty Goedicke
Heyse Klopstock Kleist
Luxemburg Puschkin Homer Mörike
La Roche Horaz Musil
Machiavelli Kierkegaard Kraft Kraus
Navarra Aurel Musset Moltke
Nestroy Marie de France Lamprecht Kind Kirchhoff Hugo
Laotse Ipsen Liebknecht
Nietzsche Nansen Ringelnatz
Marx Lassalle Gorki Klett Leibniz
von Ossietzky May vom Stein Lawrence
Irving
Petalozzi Knigge
Platon Pückler Michelangelo Kafka
Sachs Poe Liebermann Kock
de Sade Praetorius Mistral Zetkin Korolenko

The publishing house tredition has created the series **TREDITION CLASSICS**. It contains classical literature works from over two thousand years. Most of these titles have been out of print and off the bookstore shelves for decades.

The book series is intended to preserve the cultural legacy and to promote the timeless works of classical literature. As a reader of a **TREDITION CLASSICS** book, the reader supports the mission to save many of the amazing works of world literature from oblivion.

The symbol of **TREDITION CLASSICS** is Johannes Gutenberg (1400 – 1468), the inventor of movable type printing.

With the series, tredition intends to make thousands of international literature classics available in printed format again – worldwide.

All books are available at book retailers worldwide in paperback and in hardcover. For more information please visit: www.tredition.com

tredition was established in 2006 by Sandra Latusseck and Soenke Schulz. Based in Hamburg, Germany, tredition offers publishing solutions to authors and publishing houses, combined with worldwide distribution of printed and digital book content. tredition is uniquely positioned to enable authors and publishing houses to create books on their own terms and without conventional manufacturing risks.

For more information please visit: www.tredition.com

The Annual Catalogue (1737) Or, A New and Compleat List of All The New Books, New Editions of Books, Pamphlets, &c.

J. Worrall

Imprint

This book is part of the TREDITION CLASSICS series.

Author: J. Worrall
Cover design: toepferschumann, Berlin (Germany)

Publisher: tredition GmbH, Hamburg (Germany)
ISBN: 978-3-8495-0557-8

www.tredition.com
www.tredition.de

THE

PREFACE.

AS all Lovers of Literature, are pleased to know what Works are published; the following LIST was principally intended, for those Gentlemen, Ladies, &c. who live remote from London, or seldom see the Multitude of News-Papers, wherein Books are advertised; that they might for a small Expence see what B O O K S have been publish'd in the Preceeding Year 1736. And what makes this Tract farther Useful, is, I have printed the Titles of the B O O K S Alphabetically, and distinguished the Booksellers Name in Italic, *each Book is printed for, and its Price.*

Therefore 'tis hoped the Variety this Tract affords, will yield something to please every Reader, which will be grateful to

The Editor.

[Just publish'd.]

Gallick Reports: Or, A Collection of Criminal Cases adjudg'd in the Courts of Judicature in France.

In which is Comprized,

An Account of Arnold du Tilh, an Impostor, who deceived a Man's Wife and Relations, and puzzled, for a long Time, the Parliament of France. Memoirs of the famous Madam de Brinvilliers, who poisoned her Father, and two Brothers, and attempted the Life of her Sister, &c. The Misfortunes of the Sieur d' Anglade, condemn'd (tho' Innocent) to the Gallies, and who died before his Innocence was discovered. The Intrigues of Cardinal Richlieu for the Destruction of Urban Grandier, a Priest, whom he caused to be burnt for Sorcery. The Case of Madam Tiquet, beheaded in the late Reign, for attempting the Life of her Husband.

To which is prefixed a copious Preface, in Relation to the Laws and Constitution of France.

[Pg 1]

ABrabanal's (Sol.) complaint of the Children of Israel, representing their Grievance under the Penal-Laws, and praying, that if the Tests are repealed, the Jews may have the Benefit of this Indulgence, &c. *6d.*

Abridgement (A new) of the Law, 2 vols. Sold by *H. Lintot, 2l. 10s.*

Abridgement of the Statutes from the 4th to the 9th Years of King *George* IId, inclusive, being Vol. the 9th, *R. Gosling, 4s. 6d.*

Abstracts of the Act for Building the Bridge at Westminster. To which are added, Terms of Insurance, &c. *J. Millan, 1s.*

Abstracts of the Acts of the 8th Year of K. George IId, *J. Baskett, 3s. 6d.*

Acis and Galatea; A Pastoral Opera, *J. Osborne, 6d.*

Addison's Dissertation on the most celebrated Roman Poets, *J. Wilford, 2s.*

Address to the People; occasioned by an Insult upon some late Acts of Parliament, *J. Roberts, 3d.*

Adventures of Eovaai, Princess of Ijavio, a Pre-Adamitical History, &c. *S. Baker, 2s. 6d.*

Advice of a Mother to her Son and Daughter, 2d Edit. *T. Owen, 1s.*

Advice to a Friend on his Marriage, *T. Cooper, 1s.*

Advice of a Mother to her Son and Daughter, publish'd in France and Holland, with great Applause, *T. Worrall, 2s.*

Ainsworth's (Rob.) Thesaurus Linguæ Latinæ, Compendiarius: Or, A Compendious Dictionary of the Latin Tongue, Mess. *Knapton,* &c. *18s.* [Pg 2]

Ainsworth's natural and easy Way of Institution, by making a domestic Education less chargeable to Parents, &c. *J. Wilford, 1s.*

Alberoni's (Card.) Scheme for reducing the Turkish Empire to the Obedience of Christian Princes, &c. *J. Roberts, 1s. 6d.*

Allen's (William) Ways and Means to raise the Value of Land: Or, The Landlord's Companion, &c. *J. Roberts, 1s.*

Alliance (The) between Church and State: Or, The Necessity of an Establish'd Religion, &c. *F. Gyles, 2s.*

Alzire: Or, Les Americains, Tragedie A Paris, 1736, *J. Nourse, 1s. 6d.*

Alzira, a Tragedy from the Fr. *J. Osborne, 1s. 6d.*

Anacreon's Works, Greek and English, with Notes, *J. Osborne, 3s.*

Anderson's (Jam.) Royal Genealogical Tables of Emperors, Kings and Princes, from Adam to these Times, &c. *C. Davis, 1l. 16s.*

Answer to the Country Parson's Plea, against the Quakers Tythe-Bill, *J. Roberts, 1s.*

Answer to a Pamphlet entituled, An Apologetical Defence of a Book entituled, A plain Account of the Lord's Supper, *J. Roberts, 3d.*

Answer (An) to a late Pamphlet, entituled, An Examination of the Scheme of Church Power, laid down in the Codex Juris Ecclesiastici, Anglicana, &c. *J. Roberts, 2s.*

Vid. Notes on an Answer, Post.

Antiquities explained: Being a Collection of figured Gems from the Classicks, Mess. *Knapton, 10s.*

Apology (An) for the Ministers of State; Or, The Rudiments of Modern Patriotism, *6d.*

Arbiter's (Petronius) Works, translated into English, by Mr Addison, *J. Osborne, 3s.*

Ariosto's (Lud.) Satires and Poems, with the Author's Effigie, *O. Payne, 3s. 6d.* [Pg 3]

Art (The) of Pleasing in Conversation, French and English, 2 Vols. *W. Feales, C. Corbett, &c. 6s.*

Ascough's (Sir Fran.) Sermon preached before the Hon. House of Commons at Westminster, Jan. 30, 1736, *T. Osborne, 1s.*

Athanasian Forgeries, &c. collected chiefly out of Mr Whiston's Writings, by a Lover of Truth; 2 Narratives of Mr Jackson's being refus'd the Sacrament at Bath, *J. Noon, 3d.*

Atkins's Navy Surgeon, 2d Edit. Mess. *Ward* and *Chandler, 3s.*

Atkins's (John) Voyage to Guinea, Brasil, &c. *C. Ward, R. Chandler, 4s.*

Atkins's (John) Vertues and Uses of Cold and Hot Mineral Springs in general, particularly those of Scarborough, *A. Dodd, 1s.*

Atkinson's (T.) Conference between a Painter and an Engraver, containing Instructions for young Artists, *6d.*

Attorney and Pleader's Treasury: Containing the Forms of the most useful Pleas in Abatement, and in Bar, &c. 2 Vols. *R. Gosling, 12s.*

Augustini's (M.) sure Method to bring Sight to the Eyes, to those who never had it; and to restore it to those who by any Accident have lost it, &c. Sold next Door to John's Coffee-house, St Martin's Lane.

B.

Bacon's (Ld.) Law Tracts: Containing his Elements, Read. on the Stat. Uses, &c. *R. Gosling, 5s.*

Bailey's Dictionarium Britannicum: Or, A more compleat English Dictionary than any yet extant, with 500 Cuts, 2d Edit. *T. Cox, 1l. 5s.*

Bailey's (N.) Dictionarium Domesticum: Being a new and compleat Household Dictionary, *C. Hitch, 6s.* [Pg 4]

Bailey's Æsopian Fables of Phædrus Augustus, Cæsar's Freedmen, *D. Browne, 2s.*

Ball's Remarks on a new Way of Preaching, *A. Dodd, 3d.*

Barton's (Phil.) Sermon preached before the Sons of the Clergy at St Paul's, 19 Feb. 1736, *T. Wotton, 6d.*

Barwick's (Dr John) Life, with his Effigies, written by his Brother, Dr Pet. Barwick, *C. Davis, 5s.*

Batrachomuomachia: Or, The Battle of the Frogs and Mice, from Homer, *J. Wilford, 6d.*

Bayle's (Mons.) Historical and Critical Dictionary, Nº 82 to Nº 110, each *1s.*

Beau's Miscellany: A Collection of Amorous Tales, Poems, Songs, &c. 2 Parts, *J. Worrall,* each *1s.*

Beau (The) Philosopher, a Poem by a Gentleman of Cambridge, *J. Roberts, 1s. 6d.*

Beggar's (The) Pantomine: Or, The Contending Colombines, *C. Corbett, W. Warner, 6d.*

Bennet's (Tho.) Dis. of Schism, 4th Ed. *W. Innys, 4s.*

Benson's (G.) History of the first planting of the Christian Religion, taken from the Acts of the Apostles, &c. 2 Vols. *R. Ford, 10s.*

Bernard's (Tho.) Sermon at Felsted in Essex, 12 Aug. 1736, before the Gentlemen educated at the two Schools there, *B. Motte, 6d.*

Bird's Modern Conveyancer, approved by the most eminent Council, viz. Sir Edw. Northey, Mr Webb, Mr Pigott, &c. *J. Worrall, 1l.*

Bishop's (Tho.) plain Exposition of the Catechism of the Church of England, *M. Downing, T. Longman, 5s.*

Blackerby's (Nath.) Justice's Companion, 2 Vols. 5th Edit. *T. Osborne, 6s.*

Bland's (Jam.) Charms of Women: Or, A Mirror for the Ladies, *E. Curl, 4s.*

Blythe's (F.) Advice to a Friend on his Marriage, a poem, *T. Cooper, 1s.* [Pg 5]

Boerhaave's (Her.) Elements of Chymistry, translated by Tim. Dallow, *J. Pemberton, 1l. 1s.*

Boileau's (Mons.) Works made English, from the last Par. Ed. with Cuts, 3 Vols, *E. Littleton, 15s.*

Bolde's (Sam.) Help in Devotion: Or, The New Test. considered, *R. Hett, 1s. 6d.*

Boston's (Tho.) View of the Covenant of Grace, from the Sacred Rec. &c. *J. Davidson, 4s. 6d.*

Bounce to Fop, an Heroic Epistle from a Dog at Twitenham to a Dog at Court, by Dr Sw — ft, *6d.*

Bowyer's (Tho.) true Account of the Sacrament, in Answer to a plain Account, &c. *C. Rivington, 3s. 6d.*

Boyer's (A.) History of Q. Anne, Civil and Military, with Curious Cuts and Plans, *T. Woodward, 1l. 5s.*

Bradley's Country Housewife, and Ladies Monthly Director in the Management of a House, and the Delights and Profits of a Farm, &c. 2 Pts. *D. Browne, each Stitch'd 2s. 6d.*

Bradley's Riches of a Hop Garden explained, 2d Edit. *D. Browne, 1s. 6d.*

Brett's (Tho.) true Scripture Account and Benefits of the Eucharist, *J. Roberts, 2s.*

Brief (A) Enquiry how far every Government has a Right to defend itself, *T. Cooper*, 6d.

Brief (A) Representation of the Faith once delivered to the Saints, made to a Dissenting Congregation, *H. Whitridge, A. Cruden*, 6d.

Brine's (John) Remarks on a Pamphlet entituled, Some Doctrines in the Superlapsarian Scheme examined by the Word of God, *A. Ward*, 6d.

British Representative: Or, A general List of the Parliaments of Great Britain: Which are Eight in Number, *T. Astley*, 1s.

British Theatre: A Collection of Plays, 10 Vols. *W. Feales*, 1l. 10s.

Brome's (Edm.) Christian Devotion, recommended, *E. Wicksteed*, 4s. [Pg 6]

Browne's (Sir Tho.) Religio Medici, *J. Torbuck, C. Corbett*, &c. 2s. 6d.

Browning's (J.) Compend. System of Natural Philosophy, Part 2, *S. Harding*, 1s. 6d.

Bunyan's (John) Works, upon various Divine Subjects, *A. Ward*, 1l.

Burnet (Tho.) Archæologiæ Philosophicæ: Or, The Antient Doctrine concern. the Original of Things, *J. Fisher*, 5s.

Burrough's (Jos.) View of Popery, &c. *J. Gray*, 2s.

Butler's (Jos.) Analogy of Religion, natural and revealed, &c. 2d Edit. Mess. *Knapton*, 6s.

Burt's (Job.) Beauties and Excell. of Holy Baptism display'd, in Ans. to the Quakers, *J. Noon*, 1s. 6d.

C.

Cambray's (Bp.) Tales and Fables, 29 Copper Plates, *J. Osborne, 2s.*

Candidates (The) Guide: Or, The Elector's Right decided, by the Hon. House of Commons in all controverted Elections in the Counties of South-Britain, *J. Stagg, J. Brindley, 1s.*

Carey's Honest Yorkshire Man, a Ballad Opera, *L. Gilliver, 6d.*

Carmen Seculare for the Year 1735, to the King on his going to Hanover, *J. Roberts, 1s.*

Carter's (Cha.) Compleat City and Country Cook, Illustrated with 49 Copper-plates, *A. Bettesworth, 5s.*

Cartrou and Rouille's Roman History, with Copper Plates, Vol. 5th, translated by Rich. Bundy, D.D. *A. Bettesworth, 1l. 10s.*

Cases in Law and Equity, chiefly during the Time the Ld. Macclesfield presided in those Courts, *T. Ward, E. Wicksteed, 1l. 2s. 6d.*

Caveat (A) against the Dissenters, *J. Roberts, 6s.*

Celinia: Or, the History of Hyempsal K. of Numidia, 2 Vols. *E. Davis, 6s.* [Pg 7]

Chamberlayne's State of Great Britain, 32d Edit. *B. Motte, &c. 7s.*

Chamberlayne's (John) Arguments of the Old and New Test. 3 Vols. 2d Edit. *M. Downing, 15s.*

Chandler's (S.) Hist. of Prosecut. among the Heathens, Christian Emperors, Inquisitions and Protestants, *J. Gray, 18s.*

Chandler's (Mrs Mary) Description of Bath, a Poem, 3d Edit. *J. Leak.* [*Transcriber's Note: price missing in original.*]

Chapelle's (Vinc.) Modern Cook, with several curious Cuts, 3 Vols. *T. Osborne, 15s.*

Chapman's (Edm.) Treatise on the Improvement of Midwifry, 2d Edit. enlarged, *C. Corbett, 4s.*

Character of John Sheffield Duke of Buckinghamshire, with his Grace's last Will, *J. Stagg, 1s.*

Character of a Freeman, a Poem, *J. Crichly, 6d.*

Child (Sir Jos.) on Trade, 4th Edition, *C. Corbett, 2s. 6d.*

Christian Exceptions to the plain Account of the Sacrament, *J. Nourse, 1s.*

Chubb's (Tho.) Two Letters, 1. An Enquiry concerning Church Discipline, 2. Covenant, *1s. 6d.*

Cibber's (Col.) Dramatick Works, 4 Vols. *W. Feales, 11s.*

Claims of the Clergy to a Divine Right of Maintenance, &c. *T. Cooper, 6d.*

Clarendon's (Ld.) Vindication of the Conduct of James Duke of Ormond, *J. Wilford, 5s.*

Clarke (Dr) Sermons on several Important Subjects 10 Vols. Mess. *Knapton, 2l. 10s.*

Clark's (J.) Ovid's Metamorphoses, Lat. and Eng. the English Translation as Literal as possible for the Attainment of the Sense, and the Elegency of this great Poet, *A. Bettesworth* and *C. Hitch, 5s.*

Clarke's (Geo.) last Will and Testament, *J. Roberts, 1s.*

Clayton's (John) Sermon before Baron Carter at Lancaster Assizes, *C. Rivington, 6d.* [Pg 8]

Clergyman's (The) Petition for a Repeal of the Test Acts, *J. Roberts, 6d.*

Cleveland's (E.) History of the Noble Family of Courtnay, 3 Vols. *S. Birt, 16s.*

Clifford's (M.) Treatise of Human Reason, 3d Edit. *J. Stone, 1s.*

Clutton's (Jos.) short and certain Method for Curing continued Feavers, by the Assistance of a new Febrifuge, &c. *J. Huggenson, 2s.*

Clutton's good and bad Effects of Joshua Ward's Pill and Drop, in 68 Cases, *J. Wilford, 6d.*

Cobden's (Edw.) Sermon preached to the Society for Reformation of Manners at St Mary Le Bow, *M. Downing, 6d.*

Cockburn's Sea Diseases, 3d Edit. *G. Strahan, 4s. 6d.*

Cockburn's Ghonorrhea, *G. Strahan, 4s. 6d.*

Colbatch's (Sir John) Dissertation on C. Misletoe, *D. Browne, 1s.*

Coles's Dictionary, English-Latin, Latin-English, 13th Edit. *J. Walthoe, 7s.*

Collection (A) of English and Scotch Songs, Nº I, II, III, *T. Boreman, each 6d.*

Collection of Merry Poems, Tales, Epigrams, &c. *T. Cooper, 1s. 6d.*

Collection (A) of above 150 Ballads, adorned with above 40 Cop. Plates, 3 Vols. *J. Roberts, 10s. 6d.*

Collection of Epigrams, 2 Vols. *J. Walthoe, 5s.*

Colliber's (Sam.) Impartial Enquiry into the Existance and Nature of God, with Remarks on Dr Clarke on the Attributes, *R. Robinson, P. Knapton, 3s.*

Collier's (Jer.) Manual of Epictetus the Philosopher, *O. Payne, 1s. 6d.*

Collins's (Arth.) Peerage of England, now Existing either by Tenure, Summons, Creation, 4 Vols. with curious Copper Plates, *R. Gosling, 1l. 5s.* [Pg 9]

Collins's Proceedings, Precedents and Arguments on Claims and Controversies concern. Baronies by Writ, and other Honours, *T. Wotton, 1l. 7s.*

Compleat Arbitrator: Or, Law of Awards, and Arbitraments in all its Branches, by an Eminent Hand, *J. Worrall, 4s. 6d.*

Compleat Housewife, being a Collection of above 500 Receipts in Cookery, &c. *J. Pemberton, 5s.*

Compleat (The) Family Piece, and Country Gentlemen and Farmers best Guide, in 3 Parts, *J. Roberts, 3s.*

Coney's (Dr) Narrative of the Case of Mr Jackson's being refused the Sacrament at Bath, *J. Noon, 3d.*

Congratulatory (A) Poem on the Prospect of Peace, *J. Roberts, 6d.*

Congress: (The) Or, Grimace on all Sides, a Poem, *1s.*

Conjugal Duty: Or, Wedding Sermons, Pt. 1st, 2d, *J. Watson*, each, *1s. 6d.*

Connoisseur: Or, every Man in his Folly, *R. Wellington, 1s. 6d.*

Considerations upon too much Indulgence to Foreigners, *T. Boreman, 1s.*

Constable's (John) Reflections upon the Accuracy of Style, *J. Osborne, 3s.*

Cornthwaite's (Rob.) Seventh Day Sabbath farther vindicated, *J. Noon, 1s.*

Cornthwait's, second Defence of some Reflections on Dr Wright's Treatise of the Lord's Day, *J. Noon, 6d.*

Corporation and Test Acts no Importance to the Church of England, *J. Roberts, 1s.*

Country (The) Builder's Estimates: Or, Architect's Companion, &c. *J. Hodges, 1s. 6d.*

Court Kalendar for the Year 1737, *J. Watson, 6d.* [Pg 10]

Cowper's (Wm.) Charges at the Quarter-Sessions for the Liberty of Westminster, relating to Spirituous Liquors, *J. Stagg. 1s.*

Craft's (The) of the Craftsman; Or, A Detection of the Design of the Coalition, *J. Roberts, 6d.*

Crawford's (Geo.) Lives and Characters of the Officers of the Crown and State in *Scotland, T. Woodman, 12s.*

Criterion (The) of Christianity: Being the Queries proposed by the late Mr John Gonston, a Romish Priest, to Dr Knight, *J. Wilford, 1s.*

Cupid: Or, A Collection of beautiful Love Songs, with Prints of the Variety of Lovers, *A. Bettesworth, J. Osborne, 2s. 6d.*

Cure of Deism: Or, The Mediatial Scheme by Jesus Christ, the only true Religion, &c. 2 Vols. *Wm. Innys, 10s.*

Customs and Privileges of the Manors of Stepney and Hackney in Middlesex. Of Tenant's Neglect, Admission, &c. By Laws, Claim, &c. *J. Worrall, C. Corbett, 1s. 6d.*

D.

Daniel's History of France, with the Heads of several Kings, 5 Vols. *D. Browne, 1l. 1s.*

D'Anvers's (Knightly) Abridgment of the Law, 2 Vols. *S. Austen, 2l. 15s.*

Davenport's (Steph.) Description of a new invented Table Air-Pump, *Wright, 1s.*

Davys's (Mrs) Reformed Coquet, *J. Stephens, 2s. 6d.*

Dawkes's (T.) Midwife rightly instructed, address'd to the married Ladies, *J. Oswald, 2s.*

Defence of Baptism with Water, &c. *W. Innys, 6d.*

De la Gard's (Martin) Essay on real Felicity, a Poem, *C. Corbett, 1s.* [Pg 11]

Demonstratio Medico Practica Prognosticorum Hippocratis, &c. *T. Longman, 5s.*

Denne's (John) Sermon at St Sepulchres, 6 of May, 1736, *M. Downing, 6d.*

Design (A) of the Bridge at New Palace Yard, Westminster, by which an Expence 24,174 *l.* is saved, *A. Millar, 1s.*

Description (A) of a great Variety of Animals and Vegetables, &c. (being a Supplement to a Description of 300 Animals), *T. Boreman, 3s.*

Description of 300 Animals, &c. *R. Ware, 2s. 6d.*

Desolation: Or, The Fall of Gin, a Poem, *J. Roberts, 6d.*

Dialogue (A) between a Gentleman and a Banker concern. Funds, *T. Cooper, 3d.*

Dictionarium Polygraphicum: Or, The Whole Body of Arts with Sculptures, 2 Vols. *C. Hitch, S. Austen, 12s.*

Directions for a holy Life, by the Bp. of Cambray, *J. Roberts, 2d.*

Directory (The) containing an alphabetical List of the Places of Abode of Merchants and Eminent Traders, &c. in London and Westminster, and Kent, *3d.*

Discontent: Or, An Essay on Faction, a Satire, *T. Cooper, 6d.*

Discourse (A) on Witchcraft, occasioned by a Bill now depending in Parliament to repeal the Statute Anno, 1 James I. *J. Read, 1s.*

Discourse (A) concern. the Law of Inheritance, in Fee, &c. *F. Gyles, 1s. 6d.*

Discourse (A) of Free-Thinking, *1s. 6d.*

Dispute (The) better adjusted about the proper Time for applying for a Repeal of the Test Act, *J. Gray, 6d.*

Dissertat. on the Gravel and Stone, *J. Isted, 1s. 6d.*

Dissuasive from Party and Religious Animosities, *J. Roberts, 6d.* [Pg 12]

Dissuasive from entering into Holy Orders, by a Clergyman, *A. Dodd, 6d.*

Distill'd Spirituous Liquors, the Bane of the Nation, offer'd to the H. of Com. *J. Roberts, 1s.*

Divine Recreations with easy Tunes, Pt. 1, to be continued Quarterly, *C. Rivington, 6d.*

Divine Wisdom and Providence, an Essay occasion'd by the Essay on Man, *J. Roberts, 1s.*

Dixon's (Hen.) English Instructor: Or, Spelling Improved, &c. *J. Hazard, 1s.*

Doctor (The) and Bess. a Satire, *J. Roberts, 6d.*

Doderidge's (P.) Ten Sermons on the Power and Grace of Christ, *R. Hett, 1s. 6d.*

Drake's (Fr.) Eboracum: Or, History and Antiquities of the City of York, 116 Copper Plates, Printed for the Author, *2l. 12s. 6d.* in Sheets.

Drummond's (May) Internal Revelation, the Source of saving Knowledge, &c. *J. Roberts, 6d.*

Duck's (Steph.) Poems on several Occasions, *W. Bickerton, 4s. 6d.*

Duddel's (Bened.) Supplement to the Treatise of the Diseases of the Cornea and Cartaract of the Eye, &c. *J. Roberts, 1s.*

Dudley's (J.) Charge to the Clergy of Bedford; a Sermon at a Visitation held at Ampthill, 30th of April, 1736, *T. Osborne, 1s.*

Duglas's (John) short Account of the State of Midwifry, Sold by the Author in Lad Lane, *2s.*

Duppa's (Bryan) Holy Rules and Helps to Devotion, *J. Fox, 1s.*

Dyche's Guide to the English Tongue, 21st Edit. *R. Ware, 1s.* [Pg 13]

E.

Easter still recoverable: Or, A Method proposed for rectifying that great and fundamental Solemnity on which all the rest depend, &c. *J. Wilford, 6d.*

Elegy on the lamentable Death of the truly beloved Lady, Madam Geneva, *T. Cooper, 6d.*

Ellis's (Will.) new Experiments in Husbandry for the Month of April, Mess. *Fox, Meadows, Astley, 2s.*

Elwall's (E.) Grand Question in Religion considered, whether we shall obey God or Man, Christ or his Apostles, &c. *J. Noon, 6d.*

Emblems for the Entertainment of Youth, 62 Copper Plates, *R. Ware, 2s. 6d.*

England's Doom, a Poem, *R. Amey, 6d.*

English Presbyterian Eloquence, by an Admirer of Episcopy, *J. Roberts, 6d.*

Enquiry (An) into the Life and Writings of Homer, 2d. Edit. with Copper Plates, *J. Oswald, 6s.*

Epistle (An) to a Young Nobleman from his Preceptor, *L. Gilliver, 1s.*

Epistle (An) to his Grace the D. of Grafton, on the Marriage of the Prince of Wales, with the Princess of Saxa Gotha, *A. Dodd, 1s.*

Epistle (An) to the Quakers upon the losing their Tythe-Bill, *J. Roberts, 6d.*

Erasmus Moriæ Encomium: Or, The Praise of Folly, transl. by Bp. Kennet, 5th Edit. *J. Wilford, 3s. 6d.*

Essay on the Sinking Fund, &c. *J. Peele, 1s.*

Every Man his own Lawyer: Or, A Summary of the Laws of England in a New Method so plainly treated of, that all Persons may be acquainted with our Laws, *J. Hazard, S. Birt, C. Corbett, 5s.* [Pg 14]

Examination (An) of Mr Samuel Chandler's History of Persecution, *J. Roberts, 1s.*

Expostulatory (An) Letter from One of the People called Quakers to the Craftsman, *T. Cooper, 6d.*

24

F.

Fall of Bob, a Tragedy, *J. Purser, 6d.*

Fatal Conveyances of Ministerial Influence, &c. *A. Dodd, 1s.*

Father Francis and Sister Constance, a Poem from a Story in the Spectator, &c. *L. Gilliver, 5s.*

Father's Advice to his Son, to fix his Mind on Matters of Importance, *J. Roberts, 1s. 6d.*

Favourite Songs in the New Opera Adriano, *J. Walsh, 2s. 6d.*

Female (The) Rake: Or, Modern Fine Lady, a Ballad Comedy, *Mrs Coke, 1s.*

Fenwick's (Geo.) Sermon at Leicester, July 14, 1736, at the Triennial Visitation of the Bp. of Lincoln, *T. Longman, 6d.*

Fielding's (Hen.) Pasquin, a Drammatic Satire on the Times, *J. Watts,* (Vid. *K.*) *1s. 6d.*

First (The) Book for Children: Being an Attempt to make the Art of reading English easy and pleasant, *A. Cruden, 6d.*

Fleming's (Cal.) plain Account of the Law of the Sabbath, *D. Farmer, 1s.*

Fleurey's (Card.) new Ecclesiastical History translated into English by Mr Jefferies, *E. Curl, 4s.*

Fœdera Conventiones, Literæ & cujuscunque Generis Acta Publica, &c. Vol. 20, *J. Tonson, 2l. 10s.*

Fontine's (M. des) History of the Revolutions of Poland, &c. *T. Woodward, 5s.*

Foquet's Councels of Wisdom, &c. translated into English, *C. Rivington, 12s.* [Pg 15]

Forbes's (Dr) View of the Public Transactions in the Reign of Q. Eliz. 2 Vols. in Sheets *2l. 2s.*

Foster's (Jam.) Second Letter to Dr Stebbing on the Subject of Heresy, *J. Noon, 1s.*

Four Satires on National Vices, &c. *T. Cooper, 1s.*

Fourth (The) Commandment abrogated from the Gospel, *J. Roberts, 6d.*

Frankz's (Tho.) Philosoph. Dissertation on the Doctrine of Eclipses, &c. *J. Wilford, 6d.*

Frederick and Augusta: An Ode, by a Quaker, *J. Roberts, 6d.*

Free Parliaments: Or, An Argument on the Constitution, &c. *D. Browne, 4s.*

Free Thinkers, 3 Vols. 2d Edit. *O. Payne, 9s.*

Friendly (A) Admonition to the Drinkers of Brandy, &c. *M. Downing, 3d.*

Friendship in Death. To which is added Letters Moral and Entertaining in Prose and Verse, 3 Pts by the same Author, *T. Worrall, 5s.*

G.

Gallantries (The) of the Spaw in Germany, from the French, 2 Vols. *5s.*

Gallick Reports: Or, A Collection of Criminal Cases adjudged in France: Containing an Account of Arnold du Tilh, an Imposter, who deceived a Man's Wife and Relations, and puzzled the Parliament of France. Memoirs of Madam Brinvillers, who poisoned her Father and two Brothers, &c. The Case of Madam Tiquet, beheaded for attempting the Life of her Husband, &c. *J. Worrall, 3s.*

Gardener's (Wm.) Weeks Conversation on the Plurality of Worlds, *A. Bettesworth, 2s. 6d.* [Pg 16]

Garth's Ovid's Metamorphosis, 2 Vols. Cuts, *J. Tonson, 6s.*

Gartshere's (Geo.) Wisdom of the Apostles preaching; in a Sermon preached at Wigton before the Synod of Galloway, *A. Cruden, 6d.*

Gee's Trade and Navagat. of Great Brit. &c. *Cons.*

General Dict. N° 31, to 44, *J. Shugburgh,* each, *3s.*

General (The) History of China, &c. translated from the Work of Pere du Halde, by Robert Brookes, M.A. 4 vols. *J. Watts, 1l. 1s.*

Gentleman's Companion, and Tradesman's Delight, shewing the Manner of Dying, Colouring, Painting, &c. *C. Corbett, 2s. 6d.*

Geoffroy's (Geo.) Treatise of the Fossil, Vegetable and Animal Substances used in Physick, &c. *J. Innys, &c. 5s.*

Georgia, a Poem, Tomo Chachi, an Ode on Mr Oglethorpe's second Voyage to Georgia, *J. Roberts, 1s.*

Gibbs's Rules for Drawing the several Parts of Architecture. Sold by the Author in Henrietta-street, Marybone Fields, in Sheets, *1l. 11s. 6d.*

Gibbs's (Phil.) Improvement of Short Hand, *T. Cox, R. Hett, 10s. 6d.*

Gill's (John) Cause of God and Truth: Being a Vindication of the Principal Passages in Scripture, &c. 2 Parts, *A. Ward, 6s. 6d.*

Glocester's (Bp.) Sermon before the Lord Mayor at St Bridget's, Monday in Easter Week, 1736, *J. Pemberton, 6d.*

Golden (The) Fleece: Or, The Trade of Great Britain considered, *T. Cooper, 1s.*

Gratulatio Academiæ Cantabrigiensis Ausp. Frederici Walliæ Principis & Augustæ Princip. Saxo Gothæ Nuptias Celebrantis, *J. Crownfield, T. Longman, 5s.*

Gratulatio Academiæ Oxoniensis in Nuptias auspicatissim Illustratissimorum Princepum Frederici Divino, Walliæ, &c. *T. Longman, 5s.* [Pg 17]

Gravesend's (Wm. James) Philosophy of Sir Isaac Newton, explained, *J. Innys, R. Manby, 6s.*

Grey's (Rich.) System of English Ecclesiastical Law from the Codex, *J. Stagg, 6s.*

Grey's Examination of the 14th Chapter of Sir Isaac Newton's Observation on the Prophecies of Daniel, *J. Roberts, 2s.*

Grey's Spirit of Infidelity detected; in Answer to a Pamphlet entituled, The Spirit of Ecclesiasticks, *J. Clark, 1s.*

Grey's (Zac.) Impartial Examination of the Second vol. of Mr Dan. Neal's History of the Puritans, *R. Gosling, 6s.*

Grey's (Rich.) Sermon at Towcester Visitation, 2 July, 1736, *J. Stagg, 6d.*

Grove's (Hen.) Discourse concerning saving Faith, *R. Ford, 1s. 6d.*

Grundy's (John) Philosophical and Mathematical Reasons offered to the Publick, relating to the River Dee, *J. Roberts,* [*Transcriber's Note: price missing in original.*]

Grundy's Examination and Refutation of Mr Badeslate's new Cut Canal, &c. *J. Roberts,* [*Transcriber's Note: price missing in original.*]

Guarini's (Bapt.) Pastor Fido, a Pastoral Tragi-comedy, Italian and English, *R. Montagu, J. Torbuck, C. Corbett, 4s.* together, or *2s.* each.

Guyse's (John) Sermon at the Ordination of the Rev. Mr William Johnson, at Rygate in Surrey, *J. Oswald, 1s.*

H.

Hale (Sir Mat.) Historia Placitorum Coronæ: Or, The History of the Pleas of the Crown, 2 vols. *F. Gyles, T. Woodward, C. Davis, 2l. 10s.*

Hammond's Practical Surveyor, 2d Edit. with great Additions, *T. Heath, 3s.* [Pg 18]

Handel's most celebrated Airs in Alcina and all the late Operas, *J. Walsh, 5s.*

Happy (The) Lovers: Or, The Beau Metamorphosed, an Opera, *S. Slow, 1s.*

Harcourt's (Jam.) Sermon at Crukerne Visitation, Aug. 1, 1735, *W. Innys, 6d.*

Hare (Fran.) Psalmorum Liber in Versiculas Metrice divisus, &c. *T. Longman,* [*Transcriber's Note: price missing in original.*]

Harris's (John) Lexicon Technicum, 2 vols. in one Alphabet, 5th Edit. very much enlarged, *J. Walthoe,* Mess. *Knapton, &c. 2l. 10s.*

Harris's Funeral Discourses, 2 Parts, *J. Noon,* [*Transcriber's Note: price missing in original.*]

Hawkins's Pleas of the Crown, 2 parts, 2d Edit. Corrected, *J. Worrall, 1l. 10s.*

Hawkins's Abridgment of the first Part of the Ld. Coke's Institutes, 5th Edit. *T. Osborne, 5s.*

Hawksmoor's (Nic.) Historical Account of London Bridge, with a Proposition for a new Bridge at Westminster, with Designs on Copper, *J. Wilcox, 3s.*

Henry's (Mat.) Exposition on the Old and New Testament, from N⁰ 1, to N⁰ 17. Mess. *Knapton, &c.* Each N⁰ *1s.*

Hewitt's (John) Corn Dealers Assistant, consisting of Tables ready calculated to shew at one View the Amount of any Quantity of Grain, &c. *A. Bettesworth, J. Clark, 2s. 6d.*

Hewitt's Tables of Simple Interest from One Penny to 100,000 l. &c. *A. Bettesworth, &c. 1s. 6d.*

Higgon's (Bevill) Historical Works, 2 vols. vol. 1, containing a View of History, vol. 2, Remarks on Bishop Burnet's History of his own Time, *P. Meighan, 10s.*

Hill's (Hen.) first Six Books of Euclid's Elements, in a new Method, *J. Bonwicke, &c. 7s. 6d.*

Historical Registers, published by the Sun Fire Office, for 1736, four Numbers, *E. Nutt, each 1s.* [Pg 19]

Historical (An) and Law Treatise against Jews and Judaism, &c. *T. Boreman, 6d.*

History of Antoninis, a young Nobleman, left alone in his Infancy upon a desolate Island, where he lived 19 Years, *J. Roberts, 1s. 6d.*

History of Charles the XIIth King of Sweden from Voltaire, 6th Edit. *C. Davis,* 8vo. *5s.* 12mo. *3s.*

History of Prince Titi, translated by the Hon. Mrs Stanley, *E. Curl, 3s.*

History of the Ottoman Empire, from the first Foundation to the present Times, &c. with Heads of the Turkish Emperors, Mess. *Knapton, 1l. 5s.*

History of England by way of Question and Answer, French and English, *T. Vaillant, 3s. 6d.*

History of the Marshal Turenne, translated from the French, 2 vols. *T. Woodward, 10s. 6d.*

Hodgson's (Jam.) Doctrine of Fluxions, founded on Sir Isaac Newton's Method, Mess. *Innys, Motte, &c. 18s.*

Hooke's (A.) Essay on Physick, &c. *T. Cooper, 1s. 6d.*

Hoppus's (E.) Practical Measuring, made easy to the meanest Capacity, &c. *E. Wicksteed, 2s.*

Horace's Satires, Epistles, &c. done into English by S. Dunstar, *D. Brown, 5s.*

Horsley (Tho.) Horationa Prosodia sive de Metris, Horatianis, Tractatus, Aldi Manutis Expositio, *J. Wilford, 6d.*

Howard's (J.) Sermon at St Peter, Westminster, on the 24th of Aug. 1736, on the late Tumults, *J. Roberts, 6d.*

Humphries's (Sam.) Old and New Testament, recited at large, with Notes and Cuts, N⁰ 20, to 74.

I. J.

Jacob's (Hileb.) Five first Books of Brutus the Trojan, an Epic Poem, *W. Lewis, 2s.* [Pg 20]

Jacob's (Giles) Accomplished Conveyance, 3 vols. 2d Edit. corrected, *H. Lintott, 16s.*

Jacob's (G.) Law Dictionary, 3d Edit. enlarged, Mess. *Knapton,* &c. *1l. 5s.*

Jacomb's (W.) Two Sermons at Marden in Kent, *J. Gray, 6d.*

Jenkins's (Judge) Eight Centuries: Or, eight Hundred Cases, translated into English, with the Addition of a new Table and many References, *J. Worrall, 16s.*

Jephson's (Alex.) Discourse concerning the Lord's Day, in two Parts, *C. Jephson, 6s.*

Jephson's Reality of our Blessed Saviour's Miracles defended, *C. Jephson, 1s. 6d.*

Jewish Superstition inconsistent with Christian Liberty, &c. *T. Cooper, 6d.*

Ignorami Lamentatio super Legis Communis Translationem ex Latino in Anglicum, &c. *1s.*

Vendit hunc Librum Gilliverus
Cujus Insigne est Homerus.

Impartial (An) Enquiry into the Motives of the Opposition to the Ministry, *J. Roberts, 1s.*

Impartial (An) Enquiry into the British Distillery, demonstrating the evil Consequences of imposing any additional Duties, in Answer to a Pamphlet intituled, Distilled Liquors the Bane of the British Nation, *J. Roberts, 1s.*

Impartial (An) Review of the present State of Affairs in Europe, *T. Cooper, 6d.*

Infant's Church Membership and Baptism, proved to be God's Ordinance, *T. Cooper, 6d.*

Information (The) for his Majesty's Advocate against Capt. Porteous's. Also Capt. Porteous's Answer, &c. *T. Cooper, 1s.*

Instructions for planting and managing Hops, *D. Brown, 1s.*

Interest of Scotland considered, with Regard to employing the Poor, &c. *T. Woodward, 3s. 6d.* [Pg 21]

Introduction (An) to the Doctrine of Fluxions and Defence of the Mathematicians &c. *J. Noon, 1s.*

Johnson's (Capt.) Lives of the Higwayman, Pyrates, &c. 26 large Copper Plates. *O. Payne, 15s.*

Joseph, a Poem, by the Author of Friendship in Death, *T. Worrall, 1s. 6d.*

Josephus's (Flav.) Works with Cuts and Maps. To which is added, explanatory Notes by H. Jackson, Gent, *J. Worrall, 1l. 4s.*

Journey from Aleppo to Damascus, with the surprizing and tragical End of Mustafa, a Turk; done from the French, by J. Green, *J. Stone, &c. 3s. 6d.*

Irish (The) Miscellany by D — — Sw — — t, *A. Dodd, 1s.*

Iscariot (Dr) to Dr Codex, on the great Care of Tithes, &c. *1s.*

Isidora to Casimir, an Epistle, *J. Roberts, 6d.*

Ismenia and the Prince: Or, The Royal Marriage, a Novel, *E. Curl, 1s.*

Juxon's (Jos.) Sermon upon Witchcraft, July 11, 1736. Occasioned by a late illegal Attempt to discover Witches by Swimming, *J. Roberts, 6d.*

K.

Kelly's (George) Speech at the Bar of the House of Lords, 2 May 1723, in his Defence, *T. Cooper, 6d.*

Kelly's (John) French Idioms, with the English adapted; designed for the Use of those, who would speak or translate that Language with Propriety, *J. Batley, 3s. 6d.*

Kennet's Lives of the Græcian Poets; with their Heads on Copper Plates, 2d. Edit. *S. Austen,* [*Transcriber's Note: price missing in original.*]

Kenwrick's (G.) Religious Man's Companion, *J. Brindley,* and *R. Ryal, 6d.* [Pg 22]

Key to Pasquin, a Dramatic Satire, *6d.*

King's (Jam.) Sacramental Devotions, 5th. Edit. *J. Hazard, 1s. 6d.*

Knight's (Dr) Discourse on the Conflragation and Renovation of the World, &c. *T. Cox, 1s.*

L.

La Belle Assemblée: A curious Collection of remarkable Incidents, which happened to the Quality in France, 4 vols. 4th. Edit. *T. Astley*, *10s. 6d.*

Langford's (William) Sermon at little St Helen's, 2 Aug. *R. Ford*, *6d.*

Lansdown (Ld.) Works in Prose and Verse, 3 vols. Mess. *Tonson*, *Gilliver*, and *J. Clarke, 7s. 6d.*

Latham's (J.) View of the Difficulties attending those who enter into Holy Orders, *W. Parker, 1s.*

Law Quibbles: Or, a Treatise of the Tricks, Turns, and Evasions in the Law, to the Prejudice of the Client, 4th Edit. with the Addition of a Second Part; containing Precedents of Conveyances in extraordinary Cases, *A. Bettesworth, J. Worrall, C. Corbett, R. Wellington, 4s. 6d.*

Law Visions, or, Pills for Posterity, *J. Crichley, 3s.*

Le Brun's (Mr) Travels into Muscovy, Persia, &c. translated from the French, 2 vols. *A. Bettesworth, S. Birt, 2l. 12s. 6d.*

Lee (Mat.) Oratio Anniversaria in Theatrio Collegii, Regalis Medicorum Londinentium, ex Harvæi Instituto, &c. *J. Innys, 1s.*

Lediard's (Tho.) Life of John, Duke of Marlborough, &c. with Cuts, 3 vols. *J. Wilcox, 18s.*

Les Amusemens de Spa: Or, The Gallantries of the Spaw in Germany, 2 vols. *Ward* and *Chandler, 5s.*

Letter (A) to the People of England: Occasioned by the falling away of the Clergy from the Doctrines of the Reformation, *A. Cruden, 6d.* [Pg 23]

Letter (A) to a Member of the H. Commons, occasioned by a Petition from the Quakers, 2d. Edit. *T. Cooper, 6d.*

Letter (A) on the Nature and State of Curiosity, &c. *J. Roberts, 1s.*

Letter (A) to the Hon. Society of Lincoln's Inn: Containing a Defense of the Doxology to be used at the Reading the Holy Gospels, *F. Gyles, 4d.*

Letter (A) to Sir Wm. W— —m, upon the intended Application to Parliament for repealing the Corporation and Test Acts, *A. Dodd, 6d.*

Letter (A) on the Origin of the Degrees of Doctor More; particularly in Physic, conferred in the Universities, *J. Roberts, 6d.*

Letter (A) from Mr Forman to a Member of Parliament, *J. Torbuck, 1s.*

Letter (A) from a Quaker to Tho. Bradbury, a Dealer of many Words, *J. Wildbore, 6d.*

Letter (A) to Tho. Burnet, Esq; shewing that he hath used the same Fidelity in printing a Letter of Dr Beach's, as the Editors of Bp. Burnett's History of his own Times have exemplified, *R. Reily, 1s.*

Letter (A) from a Member of Parl. to his Friend in the Country, against the late Act for Retailing Spirituous Liquors, *H. Haines, 6d.*

Letter (A) to the President, &c. of Sion College; upon Occasion of the Addresses lately presented to the Bp. of London, *J. Roberts, 6d.*

Letters to a Friend in the Country, published in the Old Whig, *J. Roberts, 1s.*

Letters from a Moor at London, to his Friend at Tunis. Containing an Account of his Journey through England, observing of their Laws, Customs, &c. *J. Batley, &c. 2s. 6d.*

Letters written by Mr Pope and Lord Bolingbroke to D. Swift, in 1725, with his Lordship's Effigies and Character, *E. Curl, 1s. 6d.* [Pg 24]

Lewis's (J.) Philosopher's Stone; discovering the right Way to be happy, *J. Lewis, 1s.*

Lewis's History and Antiquities of the Isle of Tenet, in Kent, *J. Osborne, 18s.*

Leybourn's Traders sure Guide: Tables ready cast up, for the Use of Merchants, Mercers, Bankers, &c. 6th Edit. *G. Conyers, &c. 1s. 6d.*

Life of Mr John Gay, Author of the Beggar's Opera, *E. Curl, 1s. 6d.*

Life of Mother Gin, her Conduct and Politicks, *W. Webb, 6d.*

Life of William Rydock, alias Wreathocke, who was condemned for Robbing Dr Lancaster, June 11, 1735, *J. Wilford, 1s.*

Life of Osman, the Great Emperor of the Turks, 2 vols. *C. Ward, 4s.*

Literary (The) Magazines published Monthly, *J. Wilford,* each *6d.*

Littleton's (Edw.) Sermons on several Practical Subjects, 2 vols. 2d Edit. *E. Littleton, 9s.*

Locke's Miscellany of the Mathematicks, in 2 Parts, *J. Roberts, 2s.*

Lockman's (J.) Ode to the Memory of the late Duke of Buckinghamshire, *R. Dodsley, 6d.*

London and Country Brewer, Part 2d, *1s. 6d.*

London Magazine, published Monthly, for 1736, *T. Astley,* each *6d.*

London's Wonder: Or, The chaste Old Batchelor: Being the Life of Mr Samuel Wright, late of Stoke Newington, *E. Curl, 1s.*

Lord's Prayer in above 1000 Languages, *B. Motte,* [*Transcriber's Note: price missing in original.*]

Lord's Protest. To which is added, the State of the National Debts &c. *6d.*

Love Letters between a Nobleman and his Sister, 3 Parts, 2 vols. *J. Tonson, &c. 5s. 6d.*

Luck's Miscellany Poems, *E. Cave,* [*Transcriber's Note: price missing in original.*]

Luxury, Pride and Vanity, the Bane of the British Nation, *J. Roberts, 1s.* [Pg 25]

Luxury, with Respect to Apparel, 2 Discourses on Timothy, 2. 9. By a Country Clergyman, *T. Green, 1s. 6d.*

Lynch's (Dr) Sermon before the Society for Propagation of the Gospel in Foreign Parts, at St Mary Le Bow, *J. Pemberton, 6d.*

M.

Macky's Journey thro' England and Scotland, in Familiar Letters, from a Gentleman here to his Friend abroad, 3 vols. *R. Gosling, 15s.*

Mackewen's (Rob.) Funeral Sermon on the Death of the late Ld Visc. Barrington, *J. Gray, 6d.*

Macsturdy's (Herc.) Trip to Vaux-hall, a Satire on the Times, *1s.*

Maddox's (Dr) Vindication of the Government, and Worship of the Church of England, in the Reign of Q. Eliz. *A. Bettesworth, 4s. 6d.*

Maddox's (Tho.) Baronia Anglica: An History of Land Honours and Baronies, and of Tenure and Capite Verified by Records &c. *R. Gosling, 1l. 5s.*

Maffei (Scip.) Il Primo Canto dell' Iliade d'Omero aradatta in versi Italiani, *J. Brindley, 1s.*

Mallory's (John) Quare Impedit; in two Parts, with Tables, *T. Astley, J. Shugburgh, 18s.*

Maurice's (Matt.) Sermon at the Opening the new Meeting at Rowel, 9 Nov. 1735, *J. Oswald, A. Cruden, 6d.*

Mariveaux's Life of Marianne: Or, The Adventures of the Cfs. * * * translated into English, *C. Davis, 2s. 6d.*

Markham's Introduction to Spelling, 4th Edit. *J. Hodges, 1s.*

Markland's Art of Shooting flying, a Poem, 2d Ed. *T. Astley, 6d.*
[Pg 26]

Marsh's (Cha.) Poem on Christmas Day, *J. Roberts, 6d.*

Martin's (Benj.) Young Trigonometer's Guide, 3 vols. *J. Noon, 10s. 6d.*

Mason's (John) Select Remains of the Rev. Mr John Mason, M.A. *R. Ford, 1s. 6d.*

Massey's (Edm.) Sermon before the Lord Mayor, 29 May, 1736, *B. Motte, 6d.*

Mauriceau's (Fran.) Diseases of Women with Child; translated by H. Chamberlane, 7th Edition, *J. Clark, 5s.*

Maynard's (Edw.) Sermons preached at Oxford, and at Lincoln's Inn, 2 vols. 2d Edit. *A. Bettesworth, 10s.*

Memoirs of the Ancestors of her Royal Highness Augusta, Princess of Wales, &c. *J. Oswald, 1s.*

Memoirs of the Life, Travels, &c. of the Rev. Mr George Kelly, *E. Curl, 1s.*

Memoirs of Prince Titi, Part 1, 2, *A. Dodd,* each, *2s.*

Memoirs of the Life of Barton Booth. Esq; that Excellent Comedian, *J. Osborne, 1s.*

Merlin, a Poem, *T. Cooper, 6d.*

Merlin, a Poem, also the Hermitage, with a curious Frontispiece, *A. Cruden, 6d.*

Mesnager's (Mons.) Negotiations at the Court of England, done from the French, *J. Roberts, 4s.*

Military History of Prince Eugene of Savoy, the Duke of Marlborough, each Nᵒ *1s.*

Miller's (Phil.) Gardener's Dictionary, 3d Edit. *C. Rivington, 1l. 10s.*

Minute Mathematician; Or, The Free Thinker no just Thinker, &c. *T. Cooper, 1s. 6d.*

Miserable (The) State of Religion in England, upon the Downfal of Church Establish. *J. Stagg, 1s. 6d.*

Mitchell's Gratulatory Verses upon the Happy Marriage of the Prince of Wales with the Princess of Saxe Gotha, *T. Cooper, 6d.* [Pg 27]

Modern Cook, Vid. Chapelle.

Modern Matrimony, a Satire, *T. Cooper, 6d.*

Modest Defence of the Opposition lately given to the Quaker's Bill, [*Transcriber's Note: price missing in original.*]

Montfaucon's Antiquity explained and represented in near 500 Sculptures, translated into English by David Humphreys, 15 Parts, 7 vols. large Pap. Nine Guineas, Common Paper Seven Guineas, *J. Osborne,* [*Transcriber's Note: price missing in original.*]

Moral Reflections on Select Passages of the New Testament, 2 vols. *W. Bickerton, 9s.*

Morris's Lecture on Architecture, Part 2d, *3s.*

Morris's (G.) Tables for Renewing and Purchasing Leases and Lives, &c. *J. Brotherton, 2s. 6d.*

Moss's (Rob.) Practical Sermons, 5 vols. *R. Williamson, 1l. 5s.*

Motto's of the Spectators, Tatlers and Guardians, *R. Wellington, 2s. 6d.*

Motto's of the Nobility, &c. *R. Wellington, 2s. 6d.*

Muller's (John) System of Conic Sections, with the Doctrine of Fluxions, Fluents, &c. *W. Innys, 16s.*

Myonoatt's (John) Nature of Religious Liberty, a Sermon at St Paul's 5th of November, 1736, *R. Ford, 6d.*

N.

Nalson's (Val.) Sermons on several Subjects, Mess. *Knapton, &c.* 5s.

Natural History of Chocolate, Vertues of it, &c. 2d Edit. *D. Browne, 1s. 6d.*

Natural History of Bugs: Of their Breeding, Food, and Climate, &c. *A. Cruden, 3d.*

National (The) Merchant: Being an Essay for improving the Trade and Plantations, *T. Osborne, J. Walthoe, 2s.* [Pg 28]

Nature will prevail: An Apology for a Darling Passion, &c. *T. Cooper, 6d.*

Necessity (The) of distinguishing Public Spirit, from Party, *T. Cooper, 6d.*

Needler's (Hen.) Works, 3d Edit. *J. Osborne, 2s.*

Nelson (Wm.) Office of a Justice of Peace, 2 vols. brought down to this present Year, 1737, 11th Edit. *R. Gosling, 10s. 6d.*

Nelson's (Wm.) Laws of England. Of Hunting, Fowling, Fishing, &c. 3d Edition enlarged, *E. Withers, 3s.*

Nesbitt's (Rob.) Human Osteogeny, explained, in two Lectures at Surgeons Hall, *W. Innys, C. Davis, 5s.*

Neve's (Rich.) City and Country Purchaser and Builders Dictionary, 3d Edit. much enlarged, *S. Birt, &c. 5s.*

New (A) Roman History by Way of Question and Answer, for the Use of Schools, *T. Astley, 3s.*

New (A) Scheme for reducing the Laws, relating to the Poor, into One Act, &c. *T. Cooper, 6d.*

New Week's Preparation for the Sacrament, *J. Wicksteed, 1s.*

New (A) General English Dictionary, begun by Thomas Dyche, finished by Will. Pardon, 2d Edit. *R. Ware, 6s.*

New Abridgment of the Law, Vid. Abridgment.

New Description of all the Counties in England and Wales, &c. *J. Hodges, 1s. 6d.*

New (The) Astronomer: Or, Astronomy made easy by Instruments, by W.R. *J. Roberts, 6d.*

New (The) Year's Gift in 6 Parts, composed of Meditations and Prayers, &c. *S. Birt, 2s. 6d.* Part the first Sold alone, *6d.*

New (The) Atalantis, with a Key at the Bottom of every Page, 4 vols. *J. Watson, 8s.* [Pg 29]

Newlin's (Tho.) Sermon at the Funeral of the Rev. Mr John Hart, *W. Parker, 6d.*

Newton's Philosophy explained to the Youth at the University at Leyden, &c. *W. Innys, 6s.*

Newton's (Sir Isaac) Real or Intrinsic Par or Exchange between London and other Cities, of the several Foreign, Silver and Gold Coins, *R. Willock, 1s.*

Newton's Tables for Renewing and Purchasing of Cathedral Churches and College Leases, &c. 5th Ed. *T. Astley, 1s.*

Newton's Method of Fluxions and Infinite Series, &c. *J. Nourse, 12s. 6d.*

Newton's Method of Fluxions, English, *J. Millan, T. Woodman, 4s.*

Nicholl's (Fran.) Compendium Anatomico OEconomicum, &c. 2d Edit. *J. Clarke, 3s.*

Nicholson's English, Scotch, and Irish Historical Libraries, 3d Edit. *T. Osborne, 1l. 4s.*

No Reason for applying for the Repeal of the Test Act, with Remarks on the Dispute better Adjusted, *J. Roberts, 6d.*

Norwich's (Bp.) Charge to the Clergy of his Diocese in the Year 1736, *F. Gyles, 6d.*

Notes on an Answer to a late Pamphlet, entituled, An Examinat. of the Scheme of the Church Power, laid down in the Codex, &c. *J. Worrall, 6d.*

Nouveau Theatre de la Grande Bretagne: Or, Views in Perspective Views, of Noblemens and Gentlemen's Seats in England and

Wales, 300 Copper Plates, 4 vols. Royal Paper, *J. Brindley, C. Corbett*, &c. in Sheets, *6l. 6s.*

Numerus Infaustus: A short View of the Unfortunate Reigns of K. William 2d, Henry 2d, Edward 2d, Richard 2d, Charles 2d, James 2d, the 2d Edit. with Notes, *J. Roberts, 1s.*

Nunnery Tales from the French Manuscript, 2d Ed. *M. Lovemore, 2s.* [Pg 30]

O.

Observations on the Report of the Committee for Building a Mansion House for the Ld Mayor of London, *6d.*

Occasional Remarks upon the Act for laying a Duty on the Retailers of Spiritous Liquors, &c. *A. Dodd, 6d.*

Odell's Ode, sacred to the Nuptials of their R. Highnesses, the Prince and Princess of Wales, *6d.*

OEconomy (The) of Love, a Poetical Essay, *T. Cooper, 1s.*

Ogilby and Morgan's Pocket Book of Roads, in England and Wales, 8th Edition, *L. Gilliver, 1s. 6d.*

Oration (An) made upon Nov. 30, 1736, to a Friendly Society of Military Members, *E. Davis, 3d.*

Orders and Resolutions of the Hon. H. of Com. on Controverted Elections, *J. Stagg, 3s.*

Ordinary of Newgate's Account of the Behaviour, and dying Words of Thomas Reynolds, executed at Tyburn, July 26, for cutting down Ledbury Turnpike, *J. Applebee, 6d.*

Origin (The) of the Bath. To which is added the Wrinkle, a Burlesque, *T. Cooper, 6d.*

Ovid's Epistles and Amours translated into English Verse, by Mr Dryden, &c. with Cuts, *J. Tonson, 3s.*

Owen's Britannia Depicta: Or, Ogilby Improved, printed from Copper Plates, *T. Bowles, 10s.*

Ozinde's Practical French Grammar, in a new Method, *T. Vaillant* &c. *5s.* [Pg 31]

P.

Palladio Londinensis, Vid. Salmon.

Papers relating to the Quakers Tythe Bill: With the Country Parson's Plea against it, &c. *6d.*

Parricide, (The) a Tragedy, *J. Walthoe, 1s. 6d.*

Pardie's (J.) Essay on the German Texts and Old-print Alphabets, useful for Engravers, &c. *1s.*

Pasquin, a Drammatick Satire on the Times, *1s. 6d.*

Passeran's (Count) Twelve Discourses, Moral, Historical, and Political, for which the Author was burnt, *J. Wilford,* stitch'd, *3s.*

Passeran's Comical and true Account of the modern Canibals Religion, *J. Wilford, 4s.*

Pathetick (A) Address to the Dissenting Laity, in relation to the Test-Act, *6d.*

Patriot: (The) Being a Dramatick History of the Life and Death of the first Prince of Orange, &c. *J. Roberts, 1s. 6d.*

Pausanias and Aurora: Being the Conclusion of Pr. Titi's History, *E. Curl, 3s.*

Perzonei's (Vin.) Vindication of Mr Lock, from Scepticism, *J. Knapton, 1s. 6d.*

Persian Letters, translated from the French, by Mr Ozell, 2 vols. *J. Tonson, 5s. 6d.*

Petronius Arbiter, in Prose and Verse, by Mr Addison, *J. Osborne, 3s.*

Philemon to Hydaspes, a Conversation upon the Subject of False Religion, *J. Roberts, 1s.*

Philomelia: Or, Poems by Mrs Eliz. Singer, (now Rowe) *E. Curl, 3s.*

Philosophical Transactions, N° 436, to 439, inclusive, *W. Innys,* each *1s.* [Pg 32]

Philosophical Transactions abridged, from the Year 1719, to 1733, by John Eames and John Martyn, *J. Brotherton, W. Meadows,* &c. *1l. 10s.*

Pickworth's (Hen.) true Relation of 500 false Prophecies, and pretended Divine Revelations of the Pleople called Quakers, of a most Seditious Nature, *J. Wilford, 1s. 6d.*

Pilulæ Wardeanæ, Dissectio & Examinatio: Ward's Pill dissected and examined, &c. *6d.*

Pipe (A) of Tobacco, in imitation of Six several Authors, a Poem, *L. Gilliver, 6d.*

Place's (Cony.) Remarks on a Treatise, entituled, A plain Account of the Lord's Supper, *J. Roberts, 2s.*

Plain Account of the Sacrament, compared with the Account given by Dr Lancelot Andrews, *J. Roberts, 6d.*

Plain Dealer: Being a Select Essay on Curious Subjects, 2 vols. *J. Osborne, 9s.*

Plain Man's Instructor in the Common Prayer of the Church of England, *T. Wotton, 4d.*

Plea (A) for the Sacramental Test, as a just Security to the Established Church, *J. Roberts, 2s. 6d.*

Pleasures of Conjugal Love explained, *J. Torbuck, 1s. 6d.*

Polite (The) Philosopher, which makes a Man happy in himself and agreeable to others, 2d Ed. *E. Nutt, 1s.*

Political Dialogues, between the celebrated Statues of Pasquin and Murforio at Rome, *T. Bereman, 1s.*

Political Justice, a Poem, *J. Walthoe, 1s.*

Political States for 1736, published Monthly, *T. Cooper,* each *1s. 6d.*

Pomet's Hist. of Drugs, translated from the Fr. *S. Birt, E. Wickstead, 1l.*

Pope's (Alex.) Works, with Notes and Additions, 4 vols. *L. Gilliver, H. Lintott,* &c. *12s.* [Pg 33]

Pope's Literary Correspondence, vol. 4th, 8vo, *5s.* 12mo *2s. 6d.* Stitch'd, *E. Curl.*

Pope's Letters from 1705 to 1735, *J. Torbuck, 2s.*

Popery confuted by Papists: Or, The Protestant Doctrine confirmed, *C. Ward, 2s.*

Popple's Double Deceit: Or, A Cure for Jealousy, a Comedy, *T. Cooper, 1s. 6d.*

Power, (Of) a moral Poem, *H. Lintott, 1s.*

Precedents of Examination, Warrants, Bonds, &c. relating to Bastardy, *H. Lintott, 1s.*

Present (The) State of the Church of Scotland, with Respect to Patronages, &c. *J. Roberts, 6d.*

Present State of the Republick of Letters for 1736, *W. Innys,* each Nº *1s.*

Prideaux's (Humph.) Original Right of Tithes, 2d Edit. *R. Knaplock, J. Tonson, 4s.*

Present (The) Necessity of distinguishing Publick Spirit from Party, *T. Cooper, 6d.*

Private Letters adapted to publick Use, *A. Cruden, 6d.*

Privileges of an Englishman in the Kingdom of Portugal, at the Portugal Coffee-house, *2s. 6d.*

Prognostick Signs of Acute Diseases, *G. Strahan,* [*Transcriber's Note: price missing in original.*]

Proper (A) Reply to a Pamphlet, entituled, the Trial of the Spirits, *J. Roberts, 6d.*

Proposal for enabling the Clergy to accept advanc'd Rents, in Lieu of Fines, defended, *A. Dodd, 6d.*

Q.

Quakers (The) Reply to the Country Parson's Plea against the Quakers Bill for Tythes, *T. Cooper, 6d.*

Quarles (Fra.) Emblems, Divine and Moral, Cuts, *J. Clark, 3s. 6d.*

Quincy's (John) Lexicon Physico Medicum: Or, A new Medicinal Dictionary, 5th Edit. *T. Longman, 5s.* [Pg 34]

R.

Raleigh's (Sir Walter) History of the World, with Cuts, 2 vols. Mess. *Knapton,* &c. *2l.*

Rapin's History of England, continued Nº 1, Mess. *Knapton, 6d.*

Rapin continued, *Mitchell, 19s.*

Reading's (Dan.) English Clerk's Instructor in the K.B. and C.B. in filling up Writs of the first Process, in drawing Declarations, &c. 2 vols. *J. Worrall, 10s.*

Reading's (Wm.) Sermons out of the first Lessons at Morning and Evening Prayer, for all the Sundays in the Year, 4 vols. *J. Watts, 1l. 4s.*

Reading's History of our Lord and Saviour Jesus Christ, &c. 4th Edit. *J. Osborne, 5s.*

Reasonableness of applying for the Repeal of the Test Act, &c. *J. Roberts, 1s.*

Redeemer and Sanctifier: Or, The Sacrifice of Christ, &c. vindicated, *J. Oswald, 1s. 6d.*

Religion (The) of Satan: Or, Antichrist delineated, by J.H. *A. Dodd, 2s.*

Religious Ceremonies, Du Bosc, each Nº *1s.*

Remarks upon a late Discourse on Free Thinking; by Phil. Lipsiensis, 8th Edit. with Additions, *W. Thurlburne, 2s. 6d.*

Remarks of a Persian Traveller on the Principal Courts of Europe, &c. *P. Vaillant, 1s.*

Remarks on a late Political Farce, entituled, Observations on the pres. Plan of Peace, *T. Cooper, 6d.*

Remarks on the present Crisis, humbly offered to the Present Parliament, *1s.*

Remarks on Dr Warren's Answer to a Book, entituled, A plain Account, &c. *J. Roberts, 6d.*

Reports in Chancery, in the Reigns of K. Cha. I, and II, K. Jam. II, K. Will. III, Q. Anne, 3d Edit. *T. Osborne, 1l. 5s.* [Pg 35]

Reynell. (a' Rich.) De Catelepsi Schediasma; una cum Historia Mulieris Catalepticæ, *C. Davis, 1s.*

Ridley's four Sermons on the Doctrine of the Lord's Supper, *J. Clark, 1s.*

Rinology: Or, A Description of the Nose, particularly the Bridge, *W. Webb, 6d.*

Robins's (N.) Abridgment of all the Irish Statutes, to the 8th Year of K. Geo. IId inclusive, Mess. *Knapton, 1l. 1s.*

Robinson's (W.) Proportional Architecture, 2d Ed. *C. Corbett, 2s. 6d.*

Robinson's (Nic.) Treatise of the Venereal Disease, Mess. *Knapton, &c. 5s.*

Rogerson's (Jos.) Sermon on the Death of the Rev. Mr John Platts, *R. Hett, 6d.*

Rollin's (M.) History of the Ægyptians, Carthegenians, &c. 10 Vols. Mess. *Knapton, 2l. 10s.*

Royal (The) Marriage, an Opera, *J. Leake, 6d.*

S.

Sacchia Ludus: Or, The Game of Chess, a Poem, translat. into Eng. by W.E. *A. Millar, 3s. 6d.*

Sackville's (Ld.) Antient Tragedy of Gorboduc; being the first regular Play in English, *R. Dodsley, 1s.*

Sacrament (The) of the Lord's Supper, considered, &c. *J. Roberts, 1s.*

Sacrament of the Lord's Supper explained, by the pres. Bp. of Lond. *M. Downing, 1s. 6d.*

Salkeld's Reports in the K.B. Can. C.P. and Exch. 2 Vols. 3d Edit. *S. Austen, 1l. 15s.*

Salmon's (Will) Palladio Londinensis: Or, The London Art of Building, in 3 Parts, Mess. *Ward* and *Wickstead*, &c. *5s.* [Pg 36]

Salmon's Builders Guide, and Gentlemen and Traders Assistant: Or, A Magazine of Tables, *J. Hodges, 3s.*

Salmon's (Tho.) Modern History of America, each Nᵒ *1s.*

Salmon's (N.) Antiquities of Surrey, Sold by the Author in Durham-yard, *5s.*

Sannazarius on the Birth of our Saviour, done into English Verse, *W. Lewis, 1s.*

Scamozzi's Mirror of Architecture, or Rules of Building, *B. Sprint, 4s. 6d.*

Scripture Guide to Communicants: Being the Substance of a plain Account, &c. *T. Cooper, 1s.*

Seasonable (The) Reproof, a Satire, in the Manner of Horace, *L. Gilliver, 1s.*

Second (A) Letter to Tho. Burnet, Esq; *R. Reily, 1s.*

Sedition, a Poem inscrib'd to Sir Robert Walpole, *A. Dodd, 1s.*

Select and Curious Cases of Polygamy, Concubinage, Adultery, &c. *O. Payne, 2s.*

Serces's (Jam.) Popery an Enemy of Scripture, &c. *J. Watts, 1s. 6d.*

Sermon in Snow Field Meeting House, Aug. 1, 1735, *J. Roberts, 6d.*

Sermon (A) in the Cathedral of Winchester, before the Governors of the County Hospital, *J. Pemberton, 1s.*

Sessions Papers, *J. Roberts,* each, *6d.*

Sharpe's (Bp.) Sermons and Discourses, 7 Vols. *W. Parker, 1l. 11s. 6d.*

Shaw's (Pet.) Practice of Physick, 4th Edit. 2 Vols. *T. Longman, 10s.*

Shaw's (Jos.) Practical Justice, 2 vols. 3d Edit. *T. Ward, E. Wickstead, 12s. 6d.* [Pg 37]

Short Instructions for them that are preparing for Confirmation, &c. *C. Rivington, 6d.*

Short and easy Method with the Deists, with a Letter from the Author to a Deist on his Conversion, *G. Strahan, 3s.*

Sidney's (Sir Phil.) Works, 3 vols. 14th Edition, *R. Gosling, 15s.*

Skelton's Pithy, Pleasant and Profitable Works, *C. Davis, 5s.*

Sketch (A) of the Situation of a Palace at Whitehall, &c. *4d.*

Sloss's (Jam.) Doctrine of the Trinity explained and confirmed in several Sermons at Nottingham, *J. Davidson, 5s.*

Smith's (W.) Free Mason's Pocket Companion, *J. Torbuck, 2s.*

Smith's (Jam.) Specimen of antient Carpentry, &c. *H. Lintott, 10s.*

Soame's (Dav.) Sermon on the Death of the Rev. Mr Tho. Saunders at Ketering, *R. Hett, 6d.*

Some Doctrines in the Superlapsarian Scheme examined by the Word of God, *S. Cruden, 1s. 6d.*

Some Observations on the Case of the Dissenters, with Reference to the Corporation and Test Acts, *T. Cooper, 6d.*

Some Observations on the present Plan of Peace, *R. Haynes, 6d.*

Some Proposals for the Revival of Christianity, *T. Cooper, 6d.*

Some Remarks on a Letter to Tho. Burnet, Esq; said to be written by a Son of Dr Beach, *T. Cooper, 6d.*

Some seasonable Considerations on the State of the Nation, *T. Cooper, 6d.*

Some plain Reasons offered against the Bill now depending in Parliament, to Restrain the dispos. Land, *J. Roberts, 3d.* [Pg 38]

Some Remarks on the Tragedy of Hamlet, *T. Cooper, 1s.*

Somervile's Chace, a Poem, *G. Hawkins, 2s. 6d.*

Spectacle de la Nature: Or, Nature display'd; illustrated with near 100 Copper Plates, 3 Vols. *J. Pemberton, &c. 18s.*

Speech (The) of Mr John Talbot Campbell, a free Christian Negroe, to his Countrymen in the Mountains of Jamaica, *J. Roberts, 6d.*

Spiritual (The) Crisis: Or, The Religion of Salvation delineated, *J. Roberts, 1s.*

Sportsman's (The) Dictionary in Hawking, Hunting, Fowling, &c. 2 vols. with Cuts, *C. Hitch, &c. 10s.*

Stackhouse's life of the late Bp. Atterbury, *J. Osborne, 2s. 6d.*

Stanoe's (Tho.) Seven Discourses on Prov. xxii, 6, *J. Roberts, 1s. 6d.*

State Trials for High Treason, &c. Vol. 7th and 8th, to compleat the Six Vols. formerly published, *T. Wotton, 2l. 10s.*

Statutes at large, Vol. 6th, to compleat the Statutes at large 5 Volumes formerly published, *R. Gosling, 2l. 12s. 6d.*

Statutes concerning Elections, *R. Stagg, 2s.*

Statutes concern. Poor, *R. Gosling, 1s. 6d.*

Statutes relating to Bankrupts, *R. Gosling, 2s. 6d.*

Statutes for preserv. of the Game, *R. Gosling, 2s.*

Stebbing's (Dr) State of the Controversy with Mr Foster on the Subject of Heresy, *J. Pemberton, 1s.*

Stephens's (Huster.) Italian Book-keeping reduced into Art, *W. Mears, 10s.*

Steukeley's (W.) Palæographa Sacra: Or, Discourses on Monuments of Antiquity, Nº 1, *2s. 6d.*

Stillingfleet's (Dr) Life; his Controversies, &c. *J. Torbuck, 2s.* [Pg 39]

Stirling's Corderii Coloquicorum Centura Pelecta [*Transcriber's Note: price missing in original.*]

Stirling's (J.) Satires of Persius Flacus, for the Use of Schools, *T. Astley, 1s.*

Stirling's Pub. Ovidii Nasonis Tristia, *T. Astley, 2s. 6d.*

Stirling's Eutropij Historia Romanæ Breviarium, *T. Astley, 2s. 6d.*

Stirling's System of Rhetorick, *T. Astley, 4d.*

Stirling's Paracide, a Tragedy, *1s.*

Stonecastle's Universal Spectator, 2 Vols. *J. Pemberton, T. Worrall,* &c. *5s.*

Strong's (Nath.) England's perfect School-Master: Or, Directions for exact Spelling, &c. *E. Parker, 1s.*

Summary (A) of Natural Religion; containing a Proof of the Being and Attributes of God, &c. *J. Roberts, 2s.*

Summary (A) View of Westminster Hall, [*Transcriber's Note: price missing in original.*]

Supplement (A) to the Sermons at Salters-hall against Popery: Containing Remarks on a great Corruption therein omitted, *J. Noon, 1s.*

Supplement to the Impartial Enquiry into the British Distillery, [*Transcriber's Note: price missing in original.*]

Swift's and Pope's Miscellanies, 4 vols. *B. Motte, 10s.*

Symbola Heroica; Or, The Mottoes of the Nobility and Baronets of Great Britain, *J. Stephens, 1s. 6d.*

Sylverler's (Tip.) Critical Dissertation on Tit. iii. 10, *T. Cooper, 1s.*

Syren (The) a Collection of the most Celebrated English Songs, *J. Osborne, 2s.* [Pg 40]

T.

Tale Of a Tub bottled off and moralized, *J. Roberts, 6d.*

Tendon's new French Grammar, teaching without a Master, *J. Millan, J. Fox, 2s.*

Terentij (Pub.) Afri Comædia ad editionem & Harii & Bentleij. *B. Barker, 16s.*

Testimony (A) of Antiquity concerning the Sacramental Body and Blood of Christ, &c. *J. Roberts, 2s.*

Theory (The) and Practice of Gardening. Of Pleasure Gardens, &c. done from the French of Alexander Blond, by J. James, 2d Edit. *J. Osborne, 15s.*

Thomas's (Wm.) Survey of the Cathedral Church of Worcester, *J. Clark,* Duck Lane. [*Transcriber's Note: price missing in original.*]

Thompson's Britain: Or, Fourth Part of Liberty, a Poem, *A. Millar, 1s. 6d.*

Thompson's Prospect: Or, Fifth Part of Liberty, a Poem, *Millar, 1s.*

Toleration disapproved and condemned by a Letter of the Presbyterian Ministers in London; presented to the Assembly of Divines at Westminster, 1645, *J. Stagg, 1s.*

Tottie's View of Reason, a Sermon at St Paul's, *C. Rivington, 6d.*

Treatise of the Gout, in 2 Pts, *A. Cruden, 1s. 6d.*

Treatise (A) on Virtue and Happiness, 2d Edit. *J. Batley, 4s.* [Pg 41]

Trial (The) of Mauritius Vale, Esq; in Jamaica, for the Murder of Mr John Stevens, Merchant, *T. Cooper, 6d.*

Trial of Rob. Nixon, a Nonjuring Clergyman; for a High Crime, &c. *E. Cook, 6d.*

Trial of Capt. John Porteous, for wounding and killing several Persons at a late Execution, at Edinburgh, *T. Cooper, 6d.*

Trial of Old Father Christmass, for encouraging his Majesty's Subjects in Idleness, Drunkenness, &c. *T. Cooper, 6d.*

True (A) Account of the Doctrine of Christ, and the Primitive Church, with Respect to the Eucharist, shewing the Inconsistency of a late Sacramental Piece, called a plain Account, *F. Gyles, 3s. 6d.*

True (The) Secret History of the Kings and Queens of England, 2 Vols. *D. Browne, 8s.*

True (The) Picture of Quakerism; in a View of the Blasphemies, Heresies, &c. of the Quakers of Old, *J. Roberts, 1s.*

True State of England; containing the Duty, Business and Salary of every Officer, Civil and Military, *J. Fox, 3s.*

Truth (The) and Importance of the Doctrine of the Trinity, &c. demonstrated, *J. Noon, 1s.*

Truth and Reason displayed to British Subjects, in a View of the past and present State, *T. Cooper, 1s.*

Turner's (Dan.) Art of Surgery, 2 Vols. 5th Edit. *J. Clark, 10s.*

Turner's Diseases of the Skin, 5th Edit. *5s.*

Turner on the Veneral Disease, 4th Edit. *5s.*

Turner (Dan.) Aphrodisiacus, containing a Summary of the Antient Writers on the Venereal Disease, *J. Clark, 5s.* [Pg 42]

Twells's (Leon.) Second Vindication of St. Matthew's Gospel, *R. Gosling, 1s.*

Two Conferences between Mr John Gonston, commonly called Dr Sharp, a Romish Priest, lately deceased, and William Gunbie, a Layman of the Church of England, on Transubstantiation, *E. Withers, 6d.*

U. V.

Varenius's (Bern) Geography; Explaining the Nature and Properties of the Earth, &c. translated into English by Mr Dugdale, 2 vols. 2d Edit. *S. Austen, 10s.*

Vaughan's (Wm. Owen Gwyn) Voyages, Travels, and Adventures, &c. 2 vols. *J. Osborne, 5s.*

Vindication (A) of the Bp. of Winchester, against those who ascribe the Book, entituled, A plain Account, &c. to his Lordship, *T. Cooper, 1s.*

Vindication of the Assemblies shorter Catechism; revised, &c. *R. Ford, J. Gray, 1s.*

Vindication of the History of the Septuagint, &c. *T. Woodward, 2s.*

Universal Beauty, Part 6th, which compleats the Whole, *J. Wilcox, 1s.*

Universal History from the earliest Account of Time to the present, &c. vol. 1, in 2 Parts, in Sheets, *2l. 12s. 6d.* N⁰ 1, 2, 3, 4, 5, 6, of vol. 2d, *J. Batley,* &c. each, *3s. 6d.*

Vocal Miscellany: Containing above 800 Songs, 2d Edit. 2 vols. *C. Corbett, C. Ward, &c. 6s.*

Voiture's (Mons.) Works in Prose and Verse, 2 vols. *J. Pemberton, 6s.*

Voyage (A) from the East Indies, *T. Cooper, 1s.*

Upton's (Jam.) Sermon on the Nature and Grounds of Anger, *S. Birt, 6d.* [Pg 43]

W.

Warning-piece to English Protestants, on the Growth of Popery, *R. Montagu, 1s.*

Warren's first Answer, to a Book, intituled, A plain Account of the Sacrament, &c. *C. Rivington, 1s.*

Warren's second Answer [*Transcriber's Note: price missing in original.*]

Warren's third Answer, *2s.*

Waterland's (Dan.) Charge to the Middlesex Clergy, 12th of May, 1736, *J. Crownfield, 6d.*

Watson's (Wm.) Rules and Orders of the Com. Pleas, from 1654, to Mich. 1736, *J. Fox, 3s.*

Watts's (J.) Redeemer and Sanctifier; or, the Sacrifice of Christ, and the Operation of the Spirit vindicated, *J. Oswald, 1s. 6d.*

Way (The) to be Wise and Wealthy: Or, Frugality recommended, *J. Roberts, 6d.*

Webster's Duty of keeping the Whole Law, *J. Roberts, 6d.*

Webster's (Will.) Arithmetick in Epitome and Essay on Book-keeping, 2 vols. *A. Bettesworth, &c.* each, *2s. 6d.*

Wells's (Dr Edw.) Paraphrase on the Old and New Testament, with Tables, &c. 6 vols. 4to *4l. 14s.*

Wells's Historical Geography of the Old and New Testament, with Cuts and Maps, 4 vols. 8vo *1l.*

Wells's Help for right Understanding the several Divine Laws and Covenants, &c. *3s. 6d.*

Wells's Controversial Treatises against the Dissenters, &c. *3s. 6d.*

Wells's Exposition of the Church Catechism, *6d.*

Wells's Young Gentleman's Course of Mathematicks, with Copper Plates, 3 vols. Mess. *Knapton, 15s.*

Welstead's Scheme and Conduct or Providence, from the Creation to the Coming of the Messiah, *J. Walthoe,* [*Transcriber's Note: price missing in original.*] [Pg 44]

Welwood's (Jam.) Memoirs for the last 100 Years Preceeding the Revolution, *D. Browne, C. Corbett, 3s.*

Westley's (S.) Poems on several Occasions, &c. *C. Rivington,* and *S. Birt,* [*Transcriber's Note: price missing in original.*]

Weston's (Tho.) new Treatise of Arithmetick, Mess. *Ward* and *Chandler, 5s.*

Wharton's (Duke of) Life and Writings, 2 vols. *J. Osborne, 8s.*

Wharton's (Duke of) Poetical Works, 2 vols. *W. Warner, 5s.*

Whiston's Mosis Chornensis Historiæ Armeniacæ Libri iii. *J. Whiston, 16s.*

Whiston's (Wm.) Enquiry into the Evidence of A. Bp. Cranmer's Recantation, *J. Whiston, 6d.*

Whiston's Doctrine of the two first Centuries concerning the Lord's Supper, *J. Whiston, 1s. 6d.*

Whiston's new Theory of the Earth, 5th Edit. *J. Whiston, 5s.*

Whiston's Extract out of Josephus's Exhortation to the Greeks, concerning the State of departed Souls, *6d.*

Wilkinson's (John) Sermon before the Religious Societies, Mess. *Pemberton, 6d.*

Willis's (Browne) Survey of the Cathedrals of York, Durham, Carlisle, &c. 2 vols. *R. Gosling, 2l. 2s.*

Willis's Parochale Anglicanum: Or, The Names of all the Churches, &c. *R. Gosling, 5s.*

Wilson's (Sam.) Sermon on popular Tumults, preached in Goodman's Fields, Aug. 1, *J. Wilson, 6d.*

Wilson's (George) compleat Course of Chymistry, *J. Osborne, 5s.*

Wilson's (Hen.) Navigation new modell'd, &c. *W. Mount,* [*Transcriber's Note: price missing in original.*]

Wisdom from above, 3d Edit. *M. Downing,* [*Transcriber's Note: price missing in original.*]

Woman's Prerogative, a Poem, *S. Slow, 6d.* [Pg 45]

Worrall's (J.) Bibliotheca Legum: Or, A new List of all the Law Books extant, to the present Year; giving an Account of their several Editions, Dates and Prices, and wherein they differ, 3d Edition enlarged. To which is now added a Table of the Cotemporary Reporters, from their first Publication, to this Time.

Worrall's Bibliotheca Topographica Anglicana: Or, A new and compleat Catalogue of all the Books extant, relating to the Antiquity, Description, and Natural History of England, the Counties thereof, &c. in the same Method, *J. Worrall,* One Shilling each, or Two Shillings bound together.

Worsley's (J.) Tables of the Greek, Latin, English and French Verbs, &c. *A. Ward, 1s. 6d.*

Y.

Yarico to Inkle, an Epistle dedicated to Miss Santloe, *L. Gilliver, 1s.*

Yelverton's Reports, with the Judges Approbation, translated into English, 3d Edition, with many additional References, *J. Worrall, 12s.*

Young Clerk's Assistant: Or, Penmanship made easy, 73 Copper Plates, *R. Ware, 3s. 6d.*

Young's (Dr) true Estimate of Human Life, *T. Worrall, 1s.*

Youth's Monitor. In Six Annual Sermons preached to Young People in Broad-street, *J. Oswald, 1s. 6d.*

Z.

Zara, a Tragedy, from the French of Voltaire, *J. Roberts, 1s. 6d.*

[Pg 46]

***Plays Beautifully printed, with Red Titles and Fron-
tispieces; publish'd at 6d. each, Sold by* W. Feales, *&c.***

Wife's Relief
Ignoramus
Richard 3d
D. of Guise
Refusal
Alban and Alban.
Artful Husband
Cæsar in Ægypt
D. Sabastian
Country Wit
Cleomenes
Lawyers Fortune
Love Triumphant
Jane Shore
D. Carlos
She wou'd and wou'd not
Friendship in Fashion
Love in a Riddle
Titus and Berenice
Turnbridge Walks
Biter
Ladies last Stake
Jane Grey
Oroonoko
Non Juror
Tender Husb.
Timon
What d'ye call it
Gamester
Cruel Gift
Double Gallant
Cæsar Borgia
Apparition
Xerxes
Sophonisba

Woman's Wit
Rival Fools
Venus and Adonis
Island Princess
Mithridates

Plays at 4d. each, Sold by **J. Osborne.**

TWELVES.

Wife's Excuse
Country Wife
Wife to be Lett
Country Wit
Don Sebastian
Scipio Africanus
Clouds
Britannicus and Al.
Plutus
Litigants
Tottenham Court
She Gallants
Country-House
[Pg 47] Perkin Warbeck
Electra
OEdipus
Love in Tears
Quaker's Wedding
Dr Faustus
Humours of Purgatory
Northern Lass
Scotch Vagaries
Merry Milk Maids

OCTAVO.

Euridice
Imperial Captives
Antiochus
Cæsar in Ægypt
Spartan Dame
Two Harlequins
Thomson's Sophonisba
Roman Actor

Three Hours after Marriage
Alexis's Paradise
Usurper
Love in a Forest
Lottery
Sultaness
Edwin
Mad Lovers
Wedding
Bays's Opera
Female Fop
Female Parson
Fall of Saguntum
Henry V.
Penelope
Non-Juror
Rival Modes
Philotas
Footman
Lady's Philosophy
Fatal Love
Medea
Briton
Themstocles
Heroic Love
She Gallants
Amelia
Acis and Galatea

Q U A R T O.

Scornful Lady
Valentinian
Wife for a Month
Wit at several Weapons
Woman Hater
Humourous Lieutenant
Love bleeding
Spanish Curate

Chances
Custom of the Country
Coxcomb
Bonduca
Bloody Brothers
Maid's Tragedy
Double Marriage
Island Princess
[Pg 48] Loyal Subject
Love's Cure
Prophetess
Pilgrim
Maid in the Mill

The above Twenty one are all written by Beaumont and Fletcher.

Thomson's Sophonisba
Artful Husband
Jane Grey
Perfidious Brother
Hecuba
Solon
Persian Princess
Scowerers
Ulysses, an Opera
False Count
Spanish Friar

Law Books just published; Sold by **J. Worrall.**

FOLIO.

Reports of Cases adjudged in the Time of Q. Anne, 1737.

Treatise of Equity, 1737.

OCTAVO.

Attorney's English Practice in the K. Bench and C. Pleas, 2 vols. 1737.

History and Practice of the Court of Common Pleas, 1737.

FINIS.